Talking Is Hard for Me!

Encouraging Communication in Children with Speech-Language Difficulties

Written by Linda M. Reinert, M.S., CCC-SLP

Illustrated by Emily S. Lynch

WOODBINE HOUSE 2013

For Dr. Jerry LaVoi, a dedicated, passionate graduate professor
who believed in me before I believed in myself.

And for all the caregivers of children who have speech delays,
may this book provide you with fun and practical tips
for helping the children in your lives communicate.

Published in the United States of America by Woodbine House, Inc., 6510 Bells Bell Rd., Bethesda, MD 20817. 800-843-7323.
www.woodbinehouse.com

All illustrations by Emily S. Lynch

Library of Congress Cataloging-in-Publication Data

Reinert, Linda M.
 Talking is hard for me! : encouraging communication in children with speech-language difficulties / written by Linda M. Reinert ;
illustrations by Emily S. Lynch. -- First edition.
    pages cm.
  ISBN 978-1-60613-192-3
 1. Speech disorders in children. 2. Language disorders in children. 3. Speech therapy for children. I. Lynch, Emily S., 1983- II. Title.
  RJ496.S7R448 2013
  618.92'85506--dc23
                                                                    2013021888

Printed in the United States of America

10 9   8   7   6   5   4   3   2   1

Table of Contents

Preface

There are many reasons why a child may not be talking as expected. Children's speech and language can be adversely affected by any of the following conditions: genetic syndromes (e.g., Down syndrome, Treacher Collins syndrome), autism spectrum disorders (ASD), physical impairments (such as cleft lip or palate), childhood apraxia of speech (CAS), hearing loss (including conditions caused by chronic middle ear fluid and infections), neurological conditions (e.g., cerebral palsy, epilepsy, traumatic brain injury), intellectual disabilities, global developmental delays, premature birth, drug or alcohol abuse during pregnancy, phonological or articulation delays and disorders, selective mutism, and illness.

Parents and caregivers spend the most time with children but often feel unqualified to help with speech problems. This book's purpose is to ease their feelings of helplessness and convince caregivers they can learn the skills necessary to assist young children to communicate more effectively, more efficiently, and to their maximum potential.

Speech-language pathologists are professionals with expertise in communication delays and disorders. They receive training to help children learn to communicate more effectively. The role of a speech-language pathologist is to help children reach their full potential to communicate on a daily basis. This book reinforces the techniques they model through direct instruction.

This book encourages all caregivers to raise the bar for the child who is capable of improving his current mode of communication. This book will be particularly helpful for assisting the child who understands what is being said to him, but finds it frustrating, if not impossible, to express himself using words.

There are times when communication will not involve talking. There are certain disabilities that may limit speech, but never communication! If a child is not able to communicate using words, she may be able to use gestures, eye gaze, body language, sign language, communication boards, pictures, or electronic communication devices. Caregivers know firsthand that the child with a speech delay can still communicate despite the lack of words.

This book highlights simple, effective techniques presented in a manner that allows you to get inside the mind of the child. By walking in the shoes of the child who has difficulty talking, we gain empathy. By hearing directly from the child, we gain confidence that we can help!

My hope is that this book will facilitate a greater understanding of children with speech problems, while providing some comic relief for the not-so-funny reality of caring for a child who struggles with talking. I hope the book will lead you to realize you do not have to be a speech-language pathologist to make a lasting and positive difference for a child with speech difficulties. You have all the tools you need to be a wonderful teacher. It's time to open the toolbox and begin!

Introduction

We all want to learn how to help the young children in our lives communicate successfully, but who wants to read yet another lengthy article when you can crack open a storybook?

This book is intentionally designed to look like a typical children's book—welcoming and nonintimidating! The objective is to offer an invitation to learn about communication that goes beyond the usual textbooks, manuals, articles, and handouts.

However, such a design may cause the reader some confusion.

- *Is this a children's book or is it an instructional manual?*
- *Is it meant for me to read on my own or am I supposed to read this to my child?*

The answer to both of these questions is "yes." It is a children's book. It is an instructional manual. It is meant for adults to read to themselves and learn ways to help a child who finds talking difficult. And yes, read it to children with communication difficulties as well as to children who do not have any trouble talking.

It is meant to be a storybook that teaches and an instructional manual that is fun.

Who Can Use This Book: It's as Easy as 1, 2, 3

Who?

- Parents and caregivers of children with communication difficulties
- Professionals working directly with children who have communication challenges or with their families
- Children—those with speech delays and those without

1. *This book is for the parents and caregivers,* such as babysitters, grandparents, siblings, and other relatives who care for the child. These folks are often too busy to read a whole textbook on the subject or reference an article. They have good intentions but the way the information on this subject is presented often seems cumbersome. That good information will have to wait for another day.

   The format of this book (presented like a children's story) offers a fresh way to learn. Caregivers will benefit from this book by referring back to it again and again as a welcome resource at their fingertips. It may well be the lead-in to further reading of additional books and articles on the subject.

2. *This book is for the professionals* who work with young children and families of young children, including: preschool teachers, special education teachers and paraeducators, daycare providers, speech-language pathologists (SLP), occupational therapists (OT), physical therapists (PT), audiologists, parent educators, physicians, nurses, Ear, Nose, and Throat (ENT) doctors, social workers, counselors, and therapists such as music therapists or behavioral therapists.

The child's daycare provider sees the child's struggle to talk throughout his daily routine. It is the daycare provider, along with the child's parents, who often best understands the value and importance of being able to successfully communicate in every circumstance of daily life. This book will be an invaluable means of empathizing with the child and easing his distress while encouraging greater communication.

Speech-language pathologists and Early Childhood Special Education (ECSE) teachers, a natural audience for this book, are well versed in child development. They will use this book as a perennial tool to reinforce the techniques they model through direct instruction.

Other professionals who work with young children have varying degrees of knowledge regarding speech development. They may be able to recognize there is a potential problem, but they may not be trained to determine the severity of the problem or treat the problem directly.

For example, a physical therapist (PT) may be working directly with a child to assist her in learning to walk. The PT recognizes that the child has difficulty talking and may benefit from a speech evaluation, but beyond providing a referral, she does not feel equipped to help the child with communication issues. A social worker may not work directly with a child, but he is assigned to assist a family with a child who finds talking difficult. This book is designed to be a "tool" in the toolbox of anyone who works directly with young children or with the families of young children. The PT and social worker can not only use this book to educate themselves on ways to better interact with the child but they can also offer the book to the family in need of some immediate encouragement.

3. This book is for the child. Read it to *any* child who finds talking difficult. It reflects his or her frustrations and triumphs, and will, undoubtedly, be a welcome comfort.

Read it to the child's peers in the classroom. Read it to the child's siblings to help them gain understanding and empathy as well as empower them to help. Concepts and techniques are presented in such a way that elementary-aged children can learn to be a partner in the early intervention process. How exciting!

How to Use This Book: It's as Easy as 1, 2, 3

How?
- As an instruction manual with pictures
- As a resource to loan to caregivers and share with family and friends
- As a storybook to provide an empathetic point of view and to enjoy!

1. Use the book as an instructional manual, a "how-to-help" book with the benefit of cute illustrations.

Read the simple story to yourself. The child with the speech difficulty is speaking directly to you—the reader. Listen to what the narrator has to say. Whether you are a professional or a parent, you will gain a clearer sense of what the child is experiencing. This is the first step in helping the child communicate more effectively.

Whenever a particular part of the storyline sounds like the child you are thinking of or working with, you can reference more detailed instruction in the *Tips and Techniques* section at the back of the book. Share these specific ideas with others who want to help the child. (Be sure to also check out the Appendices located at the back of the book.)

Not all the tips and techniques will apply to your child, but reading them may help you identify ways to help other children with similar communication difficulties. You can easily reference your "how-to-help" manual any time you need a refresher. It will be disguised as a delightful, illustrated children's book.

2. *Use the book as a resource to give* to parents, early childhood educators, and anyone who may benefit from the information within. Speech-language pathologists will want to suggest their clients purchase their own copies so the work done during their private sessions can be generalized and built upon at home and in the community. They may ask that the family share the information with other family members or daycare providers.

- Clinics and therapists may wish to have copies available in their waiting rooms.
- Pediatricians may want to keep a copy or two on hand to show parents during office visits.
- A daycare provider may find that offering the family a copy of the book to read may open the door to further discussion about the child's needs.
- Parents may find that relatives are more receptive to advice if they can read it as a children's book with an inviting format.
- Early childhood educators may discover that reading the book to their class provides an effective way to address individual differences and encourage acceptance and understanding of peers with speech delays.

Offering professional advice requires sensitivity. This book allows good information to reach a myriad of readers by many means:

- adults reading it on their own,
- adults reading it to children in classrooms,
- siblings reading it on their own or to younger siblings, and
- adults reading it to the individual child with communication delays.

3. *Use the book as a storybook for children.* Read the text that corresponds to the illustrations. The child in the story will be speaking in the first person. Simply read the book word-for-word as you would any other children's book. If you choose, you can point out the emotions and thoughts of the children in the book. The reader and the listeners will gain knowledge about children with speech delays and learn ways to help them communicate. There does not need to be any further dialog or reference made to other parts of the book.

Another variation involves using the "Talk to the Child" sections in the sidebars on each page of the story. These provide prompts for the adult who may want to engage the child more directly. The "Talk to the Child" boxes offer additional information about the child in the story. The child is not required to respond in order for this to be useful. It may encourage some discussion with siblings or peers in a classroom.

At home, the discussion may center around what other sign language words the siblings know or want to learn. The reader may encourage classroom peers to name favorite songs or lead a song that they all know. The reader can point out how we all have things we are learning and working to get better at. The reader might ask for examples of things, other than talking, that might be hard for children, such as riding a bike or buttoning buttons. The "Talk to the Child" boxes are meant to jumpstart further discussion as the teacher or caregiver wishes.

Older children, including siblings, may benefit from reading the *Tips and Techniques* and additional information offered in the Appendices.

My Family Is Brilliant!

The big people in my life are very smart! My mom can figure out what I want without me saying a word! I can drink all my milk and Dad just notices my empty cup and refills it. Sometimes I have to bang my cup on the table, but my daycare provider knows to give me more to drink.

At Nana and Papa's house, I just stand by the closet door. Papa knows I want to go outside, and he hands me my coat. Nana never lets me go hungry. I eat my pudding all gone and Nana always says, "Do you want more pudding?" All I need to do is smile and I get more pudding!

Talking is hard for me, but I don't have to worry because the big people in my life are brilliant. I think they can read my mind!

Talk to the child:

This little girl does not need to talk because all the big people in her life know what she is thinking. But maybe she wants to talk. Maybe they *don't* know what she is thinking! Maybe she just needs some help talking. What do you think? Do you think she would like to talk sometimes?

See Tips and Techniques I: Seek Advice (p. 28)

Did I Say Brilliant?

What is happening? I drank all my milk—it is obviously all gone—and I even show my mommy my cup. Do you know what she does? She shrugs her shoulders and asks, "Do you want something?" Can't she *see* I want milk?

Papa sees me standing by the door and he raises his arms and asks, "What do you want?" Papa, you *know* I want to go outside!

Nana does not even *notice* that my chicken nuggets are all gone. Hey, look at my plate!

I give Daddy a box of crayons to open and he just thanks me for the box.

What do they want me to do? *Say something?*

Talking is not easy for me! They tell me I can use my hands for talking. They have learned some sign language, so they tell me, "Talk with your hands, like this." I have a board with pictures on it and they ask me to point to the thing I want. They say it's okay if I try to say something even if it doesn't sound quite right. I could sign *coat*, I could say "mmm" for *milk*, or use my pictures…but I think I'll just go get it *myself!*

Talk to the child:

Talking is hard for kids sometimes. This little boy thinks talking is too much work! He is not happy about that. I think people want to help him with talking. He can use "talking hands" or use his picture cards if talking with his mouth is too hard. The big people can help him with talking and then he won't be mad or sad.

See Tips and Techniques II: Expect Communication (p. 28)

They Have Rearranged the House!

I cannot reach the cookie jar anymore.

I cannot get the door unlocked.

My coat is way up high on a hook.

My snack is in a kid-proof container!

Pointing, crying, whining, grunting, and pouting don't seem to work like they used to!

Tantrums just make me feel sad and worn out.

I cannot do everything for myself. I don't get it. It used to be so much easier *not* to talk.

Now I wonder if talking just might be easier.

Talk to the child:

Sometimes it is too hard for kids to get things for themselves. When talking is hard, we don't know how to say what we want. This little boy wants a cookie but he can't say *cookie*. He used to climb on a chair to reach the cookie jar on the counter. Now it is up too high. His mommy thinks he is smart and can learn to sign *cookie* and also say *cookie*. This little boy should try his words and his signs. Do you think he'll get a cookie?

See Tips and Techniques III: Create a Natural Need to Talk (p. 29)

Sign Language *Is* Talking!

Kids learn to talk by hearing someone else talk. I try to imitate what I hear but sometimes I can't make it sound like a word. Now I know another way to talk. I can talk with my hands! It is called sign language. I know how to say *milk, go, help, more, stop, eat, all done,* and *apple* using my hands. Sometimes sign language makes talking with my mouth easier because I feel more relaxed. I *know* everyone will understand what I want because I'm not just telling them, I'm showing them too.

Talking with my hands makes me feel like a big kid. I don't have to cry or whine. My family helps me learn new signs. I like to learn new words. It's fun! I'm even learning to sign big words like *hamburger* and *dinosaur*. It feels good that my family knows I am smart. I can learn signs faster than Daddy can!

Talk to the child:

We can talk with our hands. Do you know how to do that? It's called sign language. I think that little girl is happy to talk with her hands. No more whining! Let's try those signs: *cracker, apple.* Which do you think she will pick?

See Tips and Techniques IV: Use Sign Language (p. 29)

Sometimes I Need a Boost

Once my family went to a parade. I couldn't see over the big people in front of us so my daddy gave me a boost. He lifted me up high on his shoulders so I could see better.

When I can't say words with my mouth, my family and teachers give my talking a boost. They show me another way to say things, like with sign language, picture boards, tablet computers, and other devices. They call this augmentative and alternative communication, or AAC for short. These tools boost my talking!

Talk to the child:

Pointing to pictures or pressing a button are not exactly the same as talking, but they are good ways to communicate too. Everybody needs a boost sometimes, right? It looks like this girl uses pictures and a switch to tell her teacher what she wants to say. Can you do that?

See Tips and Techniques V: Offer Extra Support—AAC (p. 30)

Imitating Is a Tough Job!

I learn words by listening to you say them. I try hard to imitate what I hear. I cannot imitate big words like *helicopter*, and sometimes I can't even imitate little words like *up*. Big people tell me to "Say *mommy*" or "Say *bye-bye*." Believe me, I wish I could!

The more you want me to talk, the less I seem able to. Sometimes when I am relaxed I can say words easily—I just never know when that will happen. People might think I'm being stubborn when I cannot say a word that I've said before. That makes me feel sad.

The best way to help me is to imitate *me!* When I start making sounds, then I can usually do it again, so let's practice those. If I say "uh-oh," we could have fun saying "uh-oh" for lots of turns. If you can guess what word I'm trying to say, say it back to me so I can get better at my words.

It is nice when you respond to my words without asking me questions. It is nice when you just add to my talking. Talking is hardest for me when people put me on the spot.

Talk to the child:

It is so fun to hear children say new words. But sometimes it is not so easy for kids to say those words when they feel pressure to talk. Do you ever feel like it is hard to talk when someone wants you to? It will get easier with practice.

*See Tips and Techniques VI: No Pressure Practice (p. 30)

They Are Slow!

Papa asked me if I wanted to go out or stay in. I thought he could figure out I wanted to go out since I was standing by the door pointing. I should have known better! Again, he asks, "Stay in or go out? In or out?" And then he WAITED for me to say something. He patiently stood there looking at me to answer, "in" or "out."

I figured I could outwait Papa. He always answers his own questions. He used to say, "Do you want to go outside? Okay, here's your coat." Now he's still waiting. I don't have time for this! I finally say "Ou" and point to the backyard and Papa opens the back door!

It is not easy for me to talk, but it is *VERY* hard for me to wait. Papa might have waited all day!

Talk to the child:

Sometimes we need extra time to say things. This little boy has a grandpa who will wait for him to say "out" to go outside. Papa loves to talk to this little boy—he will wait for the little boy to take his talking turn!

See Tips and Techniques VII: Wait with Anticipation (p. 31)

It's My Turn!

Big kids, like my sister and brother, are better at talking than me. They tell Mommy and Daddy what I want. They know a lot about me and they talk for me. I like it when big people let me have my talking turn. Maybe I will talk with my hands or maybe I will use my words. I need practice. If talking was easy for me, I would tell them it is *my* turn to talk!

Talk to the child:

The little brother needs more practice with his talking. It's important that everyone has their turn to talk. The brother and sister are taking turns rolling a ball. That is a fun way to take turns too!

See Tips and Techniques VIII: Take Turns (p. 31)

They Respect Me!

I used to have no say in what I would get. Now Mom asks me, "Do you want milk or juice?" "In or out?" "The puppy book or the car book?" "Cracker or cookie?" Choices!

I like that idea—I have some control! But wait, Mom thinks I am smart. I point to the juice and she expects me to do more than point. She says, "Which one? Use your talking hands or your communication device. Use your words. Tell me—juice or milk?" Can I *do* that?

Did she forget talking is not easy for me? I want juice but I can't quite say it. I can say "du" and now I know the sign for juice. I use my talking hands and my words. I try it. "Du." Mom is so proud of me! She says, "Sure, you can have juice! I know what you meant. You used your words!"

Nana asks me, "Pudding or beans?" Nana thinks I am smart, too. I will say "pudding" as best I can and make sure it sounds nothing like "beans." "Pu-ee," I say. She understands! She says, "Oh, you picked pudding. Here you go."

I don't have to say my words perfectly. It seems all I have to do is try. Maybe I will talk more tomorrow.

Talk to the child:

It is nice to have choices. This little girl gets to choose a snack. Do you think it is fun to pick out books or choose which color shirt to wear?

See Tips and Techniques IX: Offer Choices (p. 32)

They Use My Kind of Language!

Daddy used to talk in great big sentences. I know he is smart and I usually understand most of what he says.

Mommy sometimes says nineteen words at a time—in one breath! "I want you to go upstairs and get your pajamas on and then we will read a bedtime story."

All of a sudden, they talk in kid-size sentences. Now I hear, "Go upstairs. Up the stairs. Up, up, up. Time for jammies. Jammies on. Then book time. Pick a book!" It is so much easier for me to pay attention. It is easier for me to understand them. Sometimes they even sing songs. I love it when they sing the words. The best part about the big people in my life using kid-size sentences is that I think someday I will be able to repeat exactly what they say! "Up, up, up. Jammies. Read book!"

Talk to the child:

The little girl likes to hear kid-size sentences. It is easier for her to repeat things when her Mommy talks to her this way. The little girl might say "up, up, up" or "nigh-nigh" or "book."

See Tips and Techniques X: Make it Attainable (p. 32)

Music Makes My Heart Sing!

I love music! It is easier for me to join in and sing sounds or words with other people than by myself. I get to say fun sounds over and over and over when we sing. Singing helps me learn new words, too!

At daycare, we sing lots of songs. Big people sing parts of the song and I get to finish. They stop right before the last word and I fill it in. "Twinkle, twinkle, little _____. How I wonder what you _____. Up above the world so _____. Like a diamond in the _____. Twinkle, twinkle, little _____. How I wonder what you _____." My words are not perfect and sometimes they sound more like vowels. It is okay for big people. It is okay for me!

Papa has the most fun. He sings about cookies. I sign *cookie* and I do my best talking. This time it sounds like "tu-ee." Papa starts singing "Cookie, cookie, cookie. Cookie, cookie, cookie. Hi-ho, the derry-oh—it's time to have a cookie." The best part is I can ask for "more cookie" and Papa almost always starts singing again!

Talk to the child:

Singing is a fun way to talk. This little boy likes to sing! Do you think he likes to sing about the wheels on the bus? Or maybe he likes to sing animal sounds—moo, moo, moo! woof-woof! meeee-ooow!

See Tips and Techniques XI: The Magic of Music (p. 33)

Book Time Is So Much Fun!

When my teacher Mimi reads to us at daycare, she uses all kinds of sounds. She invites us to try those sounds. I like to be a police car siren (wee-ooo-wee-ooo) and a dump truck backing up (beep-beep-beep).

Daddy reads to me with a funny voice. I like to be a bear with daddy. Grrrrr!

Mommy reads to me using the words in the book, but she stops to look at all the pictures and we make sure the pictures "talk." I especially like the creaky door (eeeeek) and the panting dog (heh-heh-heh).

My babysitter makes me laugh when she reads to me. She is always being silly. The animals make very funny sounds and sometimes she makes the story extra silly. I love it when the mouse roars or the baby makes gurgling sounds. I can always join in with silly sounds because whatever sound I make, my babysitter laughs!

Nana reads books that repeat a lot. We say things together like, "Night moon." I like it so much when she says it with me!

Talk to the child:

This little boy loves to read books. He reads at home and at daycare. He likes to make silly sounds with books. What books do you like? You can pick out another book and we can read it after this one. Books help children learn to talk.

See Tips and Techniques XII: Book Time (p. 33)

They Understand Me!

When I try to say anything now, they echo me! I say "shoe" with my words and my hands. It sounds like "dew," but Daddy understands and repeats "Shoe!" I say "hep" and "dip" for "help me zip." Mimi smiles and says, "Sure, I'll help you zip up your coat."

I tell Mommy I want a cookie and it comes out "ooty." She says, "Cookie! You can have one cookie."

I go up to Papa and sign *milk* and he is proud of himself because he understands sign language! He pats me on the head and says, "Good talking with your hands, sweetie. Let's go get some of that milk!"

I now can say "Nana" for Grandma. She likes to hear her name, so I say "Nana" a lot! If I say, "Nana eat," she will find a good snack for me. If it is a tough talking day for me, she reminds me to use my communication device or "talk" with my hands using sign language. Usually, when I start "talking" with my hands, it helps make my mouth talking easier. I like that Nana doesn't pressure me to use my words. She likes my talking hands, too! Especially when I say "I love you" in sign language.

Talk to the child:

This little girl tries to talk. It is okay if she doesn't say her words like big people. Little people can't drive cars, can they? But they will grow up and drive cars! They don't talk all grown up either—but someday they will. This little girl tries to say words. She is learning grown-up talk. She says "shoe." Can you say "shoe"?

See Tips and Techniques XIII & XIV: Accept Imperfection & Offer Empathy (p. 34)

Tips and Techniques:

I. Seek Advice

Caregivers want what is best for a child, but sometimes it is hard to know the right way to handle a situation when a child cannot communicate well. It may seem cruel to require the child to speak when the chances of success are almost zero. When we know and understand the child's struggles, it seems most kind to be a "mind reader" and circumvent any unnecessary frustration. Still, we all *do* want the child to talk eventually. No one wants to stand in the way of progress or do the wrong thing. The good news is, we want to help and we can!

Suggestions:
- Have a speech-language pathologist screen the child. (These professionals are also referred to as speech-language clinicians or speech therapists.) A good place to start is your local school district. Ask your school to direct you to early intervention services in your community. Another

good place to start is with your child's pediatrician or your local hospital or clinic. You can contact speech-language pathologists in private practice by searching your local phone book and the Internet.
- Utilize some of my favorite resources listed in Appendix H or ask your child's speech-language pathologist for their favorite resources.
- Share what you have learned to be effective with your child. Share your knowledge with other parents, daycare providers, teenage babysitters, grandparents, preschool teachers, siblings, and well-meaning friends. Give them a copy of this book.
- Relax! You have the skills to help your child communicate to his or her potential. You are not alone—your child's teachers and therapists will be with you every step of the way.

II. Expect Communication

Tempting as it might be, stop trying to read the child's mind. Consider what the next level of communication might be and expect *that*. For example:
- If the child is whining, have him point.
- If the child is pointing, have her attempt the sign.
- If the child is using a picture communication method, have him attempt a sound to go with the picture or have him expand the picture method by providing him with more choices. (Consult with a speech-language pathologist regarding what is an appropriate word approximation to expect.)
- If the child is signing, have him attempt a sound to go with the sign. (Consult with a speech-language pathologist regarding what is an appropriate word approximation to expect.)
- If the child has words but prefers to use gestures, give him a prompt of what he can say, e.g., "You can say, 'help.'"

The technique emphasized here is *expectation*. You need to expect the child to respond in a way that is just a bit more difficult than her current means of communication. Expect a response and you will be much more likely to get one.

III. Create a Natural Need to Talk

Sometimes we make it too easy for a child to remain nonverbal. We may forget that we have some healthy control over the situation. Look around and see what things you can change to create a need for the child to use better communication.

Often children who have difficulty communicating with words will learn to be very self-reliant. They push a chair to the cupboard and get the item on their own, without a word. Sometimes adults are too helpful. We fill the dinner plate and cup and set it right in front of him, never requiring the child to communicate what he wanted. In both instances, we can do a lot to encourage talking, for example:
- Hand him his shoes and wait for him to request "help."
- Wait for her to say "out" before turning the childproof doorknob.
- Put his favorite toys or treats up high, yet still in sight, encouraging him to point and sign "please."
- Put her snack in a hard-to-open container, requiring her to ask for assistance.
- Fill his cup with one quarter the amount of milk you typically would. This way, he will have to sign "more" or "milk" when he is thirsty.
- Place only one or two treats on her tray, creating a natural need to for her to say "more" or sign "eat" if she is still hungry.

IV. Use Sign Language

Some parents and other caregivers are naturally concerned that offering sign language as a communication option will replace the child's need or desire to use speech. Despite this common belief, research shows that using sign language does *not* discourage or delay speech. In fact, signing augments the process of language comprehension and speech acquisition and has many other advantages!

- Utilize sign language to bridge the gap between nonverbal and verbal communication. Children often use body language to communicate their needs. They may point, reach, or act out their requests. This does not always work, especially if the person caring for the child is not familiar with the child's particular gestures. Anyone can learn sign language. There are many kid-friendly books, websites, and DVDs to help you learn basic signs (see Appendix H).

- Utilize sign language to decrease temper tantrums and other undesirable behaviors such as whining, pouting, hitting, or biting.

- Instead of just giving in to a demanding nonverbal child, you can insist he use his hands to talk. He may not yet be able to say many real words, but we can teach him to use simple signs to give him a sense of power and control. If he refuses to sign, you can help him.

- Consciously be aware that you may be "reading the mind" of the child with a speech delay. Look for opportunities in the child's natural environment where you can require a sign rather than simply do things or get things for the child because you know what she wants.

- Let all caregivers in on your strategy. Encourage parents, grandparents, teachers, siblings, daycare providers, and relatives to learn a few basic signs. Assure them they can easily learn a core vocabulary: *more, all done, eat, drink, help, milk,* and *love.*

V. Offer Extra Support—AAC

Children learning to communicate more effectively often benefit from extra support referred to as augmentative and alternative communication (AAC) systems. Because we do not typically know a young child's potential for using speech to effectively communicate, it is important to provide AAC supports early on.

An augmentative system will support talking while an alternative system often replaces speech. Sign language is an example of both. Sign language can augment a child's speech when his expressive vocabulary is limited or when he is not readily understood. Sign language can be an alternative form of communication for a person who is Deaf or hard of hearing.

Children can also use photographs or line drawings to identify what they want to express. Pictures can be used individually or in an array on a communication board. Children can learn to offer a picture symbol in exchange for the item they desire. A young child may give a picture of cereal to an adult as a way to ask for cereal when he is not yet able to say the word or when signing is beyond his fine motor abilities.

Besides the relatively low-tech options such as PECS and battery-operated switches, there are also high-tech options such as electronic communication devices, tablets, and computers that offer speech-output capabilities, allowing children to express themselves with recorded voice. There are many apps for smartphones and tablets that are specifically designed to support communication, as well as computer programs that allow for greater individualization.

AAC can be a temporary or permanent means of maximizing expressive communication. The systems can be as simple as a picture or as sophisticated as a computer, and the systems that a person uses can grow in sophistication as his or her language grows and develops.

VI. No Pressure Practice

- Start out by playing with sounds. Just have fun with sounds while reading or playing. Think naturally: a motor of a car (brrrrm), a train whistle (woot, woot), a cat (meow), an owl (whoo-whoo), a snake (sssss), pouring tea (shhhh), drinking milk (guh-guh-guh), popping bubbles (pah-pah-pah).

- Once the child is having fun with sounds, YOU imitate the child! Instead of asking the child to "say" things after you, you become the one who repeats the child. This is the very first step toward mature imitation. The child is much more likely to be able to repeat what he just said than something new. The child takes a turn, you repeat the child, he says the same thing—and you begin a turn-taking routine where it is difficult to know who is imitating whom. Do not underestimate this important step!

- Once the child can do many turns with sounds she initiates, begin to change the patterns. If the child says "beep," you can say "beep-beep" or "honk" and see if she will change to your suggestion. When she is able to try, you can continue to offer new ideas—but follow her lead, still.

- Continue to practice those early words often—incorporating them into play and during story time or mealtime—allowing the child much practice on the words he is now good at. Do not add too many new words at first. Remember, a meaningful sound (e.g., meow) counts as a word.

- You will notice that your child is gaining confidence in being able to try new words. Whenever she seems to have a setback or a difficult time with new words, return to sound play and following her lead.

VII. Wait with Anticipation

Offering children the gift of time is a helpful technique for improving communication. When we wait with an expectant and patient look, we tell the child we have time to listen and we are confident he will be able to tell us what he is thinking. Below are some practical suggestions for patient listening:

- Wait far longer than you feel comfortable! You may need to wait longer than five seconds.
- Wait with a reassuring look on your face—an expression that says to the child, "I am listening. Take your time. I am eager to hear what you have to say and I believe you can do it!" Practice in the mirror if you need to.
- If waiting results in unnecessary frustration for either or both of you, lower the expectation to sign language, a gesture, or another form of nonverbal communication. The important thing here is to give the child her "talking turn." Her turn may be without words.
- Songs and stories lend themselves to opportunities for turn-taking practice. For example, while reading, you can make an animal noise and then wait with expectation for the child to make a noise. You can sing a song and leave off the last word. Wait with anticipation for the child to finish the verse (e.g., "Old McDonald had a farm, E-I-E-I"…pause…child says, "O.")

- Become aware of times when you tend to jump in too soon; instead work at waiting intentionally for the child to respond. Sometimes we don't realize how much we answer for our children, never giving them the chance to respond.

VIII. Take Turns

Children who find talking difficult often need more time to process the information they hear. They may hear and understand perfectly, but they need more time to formulate their responses. When we jump in too soon, the child may learn something we never intended to teach: *When people talk to me, they don't expect me to be a communication partner.* Talking is a turn-taking activity—I speak; you speak. Except, for kids who have difficulty speaking, it can feel like it's never really their turn.

Siblings, friends, and babysitters, can build in turn-taking opportunities with the child by the simple act of sharing. Peers can be encouraged to allow for turns by sharing a common playdough tool, for example. Two children baking cookies and using one rolling pin facilitates turn-taking as well. Giving children choices during meals and expecting them to respond allows them to have their own communication turns. Give them extra time to respond. Peers and older children can help the child who finds talking difficult by remembering to wait, and to not always do or say things for the child. It is okay to let them struggle sometimes.

It is important to build a turn-taking foundation in your relationship with the child. Below are some ideas to encourage you and the other important people in the child's life to be partners in communication:

- Take turns with a toy. Roll a ball toward the child and encourage her to roll it back to you. Do not expect sounds or words; simply enjoy the joy of taking turns!

- If the child is in a vocal (noisy) mood, take advantage of this opportunity for turn-taking practice. Imitate the child, repeating the sound the child made. The child is likely to repeat the sound, but allow plenty of time for his response. For example, the child pushes a car and makes a motor sound (brmmm). The adult imitates that sound, then stops and waits for the child to make another noise. The key is to let the child take the first turn!
- Refrain from filling in silent time. Ask yourself, "Have I been doing all the talking?" If so, allow some quiet space for the child. She may surprise you.

IX. Offer Choices

Who doesn't like a choice? Choices offer freedom. When a child is given a choice, positive things happen, for example:
- We respect the child's individual preferences. We let him know he has a say in the matter.
- We set up an opportunity for a natural response. It is more natural to respond to a choice than to be told, "say…" to get something.

We cannot always offer our children choices, but it is helpful to consider ways to incorporate more choices into a child's day. Here are a few suggestions that will still allow the adult to be in charge yet give the child a sense of control:
- Milk or water?
- One book or two?
- More or all done?
- Cracker or cookie?
- Mommy help or Daddy help?
- Sign by yourself or I help you sign?
- Picture card or use your sign?

Do not present choices that you are not willing to honor. If you are not willing to give your child juice, do not make it one of the choices. Be creative. Children who feel empowered by choices may be more willing to say or sign or use some other form of communication.

X. Make it Attainable

Children learn language in a very systematic way. Children generally learn language in this order:
1. Sounds, babbles, and noises that eventually approximate words (around twelve months of age).
2. Lots of single words until the child has 200 words or more (between ages twenty-four to thirty months).
3. Combining two words to form phrases such as "go car" or "sleep bed" (between ages two and three).
4. Using descriptors (e.g., hot, big, heavy) and pronouns (e.g., me, you, him) (between ages two and three).
5. Using the "little" parts of speech, like articles, verb tenses, and plurals (these skills are developed and refined over time—between ages twenty-eight months and five years).
6. Building up to grammatically correct sentences by age six.

A child delayed in talking may need more models and practice to be able to make sentences. By simplifying your sentences, you allow the child more chances to successfully imitate your model. You give the child an example that is much closer to reach. You give them confidence to try. You provide a safer environment to take the risk.

Suggestions:
- Talk in shorter sentences. Break apart your message into small "sound bites," e.g., "Shoes on. Time to go!"
- Repeat key words more often, e.g., "Time to eat, eat, eat!"
- Make up songs to sing your way through a direction (singing allows for lots of repetition).

- If the child is not yet using single words, talk in single-word sentences (e.g., "Up," "Go," "Out," or "More.")
- If the child is using single words, talk in two-word sentences (e.g., "Go home," "Bye Dad," or "Hat on.")
- The idea is to challenge the child but make the challenge reachable.

XI. The Magic of Music

Children love music. Children learn from music. It is often easier for children to join in and sing sounds or words with others than by themselves. Music also allows for lots of repetition without it seeming like drill work. Repetition in speech sound development is a key factor in facilitating accurate production (e.g., a child can practice "dee-dee-dee-dee" in a rhythmic pattern set to music far more naturally than in simple sound repetition). Music is often associated with movement, allowing children to express themselves with clapping and dancing. By bringing music into a child's day, you offer the following ways to learn:

- Through the joy it brings. It is simply fun to move and sing along to music.
- It provides lots of repetition to allow for speech and language information to really "sink in" and be learned.
- Through participation with others—music invites social interaction. Singing and dancing are very enjoyable when done with others!
- Make it up! Whenever you want to teach a child something, you can make it into a song. Take a familiar tune such as "Mary Had a Little Lamb" and replace the words to create your own word or sound practice, at a comfortable rate:

  Joey, Joey go bye-bye,
  Go bye-bye, go bye-bye
  Joey, Joey, go bye-bye
  It's time to go bye-bye!

- Music can be played in the car, or while the child is playing with blocks or playdough, or any other repetitive activity.
- There are many songs on the market geared specifically to the child with speech and language difficulties. These songs are often simplified and target speech and language skills in a developmental sequence. See the resources provided in Appendix H or ask a speech therapist for ideas!

XII. Book Time

Children's books offer several benefits for developing speech and language skills: they are often repetitive and highly predictable. Selecting books that rhyme or repeat words or phrases offers your child multiple opportunities to practice speech sounds and words. How to use books:

- Pay attention to which are your child's favorite books and read them over and over again, knowing that repetition is essential to learning language. Children love repetition.
- If a book has a carrier phrase, pause before the last word so that the child can finish the sentence. Give your child plenty of time to respond.
- Visit the library and let your child choose books with illustrations he is especially drawn to. Pause during reading to comment on the pictures. If you see a snake, try making the hissing sound together. Ask simple questions such as, "What do you think that lion says?" Explore the pictures in books to see if you can find ways to play with sound: cars revving their motors, bubbles popping, bears roaring, trains whistling, men snoring.
- Follow the child's lead. She may want to linger on some pages longer than others. She may say something about the picture. These opportunities allow you to practice speech and introduce new vocabulary.

- Children may not have the attention span to listen to books for more than a few minutes. Select board books with simple words and illustrations or photographs to start with. You can name the pictures and turn the pages at a pace that keeps your child engaged from cover to cover.
- Don't give up! If your child does not enjoy books at first, he may need more time. Ask an early childhood teacher for some book suggestions that are likely to capture the attention of a child who is reluctant to look at books.
- Consider making a photo book. The pictures can include family photos or magazine pictures. These personalized books will encourage your child to name familiar people (mama) and say fun sounds (such as "shh" for a picture of a sleeping baby).

XIII. Accept Imperfection

It is important to create a safe environment where the child can communicate naturally. When the child realizes that you do not expect perfection, he will be more willing to take communication risks. Think of something that you find difficult to do. If someone expects you to perform that skill with perfection, what will be your response? Most likely, you will not even attempt it. However, if the expectations are reasonable, you are more apt to take a risk. Children who understand language at age level may be fully aware that talking is a big risk. They think, "People may not understand me. People may demand that I say it again. If I feel threatened, I will just shut down. If the way I say it isn't good enough, I won't even try!"

Suggestions:
- Gain the trust of the child with a non-speech-related activity. Play a game that requires no response on her part. Get out the playdough and start enjoying the activity together.

Rough-and-tumble play is another way to laugh and have fun without requiring speech.
- Accept any utterance or sign in simplified form, e.g., "wa" for "water" or "moo" for "cow." Little hands cannot sign precisely. As long as the child is making attempts and taking even small risks, be sure to accept those with joy and enthusiasm. Use praise lavishly.
- Strike the words "tell" and "say" from your vocabulary, at least in the beginning. Those words tend to present a child with the expectation to perform on cue. He may resist the spotlight because he knows he is not good at talking or he may become self-conscious and be unable to "tell" or "say" when put on the spot.
- Instead of asking the child to *say something*, echo what she is able to produce vocally, even if it's not very clear. If she is able to say "sss" to indicate that the kitten is sleeping, acknowledge her speaking by saying "Shhh" or "Yes, the kitty is sleeping. Shhh." Then wait to see if she says more and echo her again.
- Enjoy the unique way the child says certain words. Childhood is a time of delight and wonder! Build fond memories.

XIV. Offer Empathy

No matter what progress we make toward our goals, we sometimes hit a rough patch. No matter how good we are at our jobs or hobbies, some days we find it hard to succeed. Think of some adult tasks that are usually enjoyable and rewarding when we do them well: golf, eating right, getting along with others. Those same enjoyable, rewarding tasks become frustrating when we are "off." A bad day on the golf course can make you want to give up the game. A day of overeating can make you feel sluggish and discouraged. When we are having trouble in a relationship, a sunny day can quickly turn to gray.

A child who has been communicating more effectively and having good success with talking may find some days to be tough. The child may be tired or ill. The child may feel pressured to improve faster than she is capable. The child may just be having "one of those days."

Suggestions:
- Remember that it is okay to take a step or two backwards some days. If the child has been using words and needs to go back to signing or using picture cards for awhile, that is okay.
- Children will plateau with a skill before they are ready to make another gain. Allow for times when progress takes a rest.
- Remember that fatigue, illness, and growth spurts can affect a child's ability to perform at his peak.
- Remember that we all have tough days and the child needs to know we love her no matter how she communicates.
- Remind yourself and your child that tomorrow is a brand new day and that this too shall pass.

Appendix A: Glossary of Speech-Related Terms, Acronyms, and Abbreviations

Professionals in the medical and educational fields often use acronyms and abbreviations to communicate efficiently amongst themselves. This can sound like a foreign language to anyone outside those fields. This glossary includes many of the terms (often abbreviated) frequently used by medical and educational professionals. The terms are listed in alphabetical order.

Laws keep changing. Research is ongoing. To obtain the most current, most credible information on any topic, it is best to consult a trusted medical or educational professional. Ask them to direct you to reliable websites and printed materials.

Another place to start is the National Dissemination Center for Children with Disabilities (NICHCY - www.nichcy.org) funded by the Office of Special Education Programs (OSEP), US Department of Education. Everything they offer on their site is copyright-free and intended to be shared far and wide. They provide numerous links to medical and educational research and news. Their introduction reads as follows: "We serve the nation as a central source of information on disabilities in infants, toddlers, children, and youth." Here, you'll also find easy-to-read information on IDEA, the law authorizing early intervention services and special education.

AAC—Augmentative and Alternative Communication. AAC supplements existing speech (augmentative) or replaces speech (alternative) when it is not functional. AAC includes such things as gestures, pictures, symbol communication boards, and electronic devices.

Adaptive Behavior—Adaptive behavior includes the age-appropriate behaviors necessary for children to function safely and appropriately in daily life. Adaptive behaviors include real life skills such as grooming, dressing, safety, following rules and routines, and getting along with others.

ADHD—Attention-Deficit/Hyperactivity Disorder. A neurobiological disorder characterized by developmentally inappropriate impulsivity, inattention, and, in some cases, hyperactivity. Although many children have these symptoms some of the time, they are much more exaggerated in a child with ADHD.

ADL—Activities of Daily Living. A term used in healthcare and special education to refer to daily self-care activities, such as eating, bathing, dressing, toileting, etc., that enable an individual to be independent in his environment.

ASD—Autism Spectrum Disorder. An umbrella term referring to a wide range of developmental disorders significantly affecting verbal and nonverbal communication and social interaction, generally evident before age three, that adversely affects a child's educational performance. Other characteristics often associated with autism are engaging in repetitive activities and stereotyped movements, resistance to environmental change or change in daily routines, and unusual responses to sensory experiences. ASD ranges in degree of severity from mild to severe.

ASL—American Sign Language. ASL is a visually perceived language based on articulated hand gestures and their placement relative to the body, as well as facial expressions, and body and mouth movements. It is the native language of many Deaf men, women, and children as well as hearing children with a parent(s) who is Deaf and uses ASL.

AT—Assistive Technology. AT is a general term that includes assistive, adaptive, and rehabilitative devices for individuals with disabilities to improve functional capabilities.

Audiologist/Audiology—An audiologist is trained in the prevention, identification, and evaluation of hearing disorders, the selection and evaluation of hearing aids, and the habilitation/rehabilitation of individuals with hearing impairment.

CAPD—Central Auditory Processing Disorder. A general term for a variety of disorders that affect the way the brain processes auditory information.

CAS—Childhood Apraxia of Speech. CAS is a speech disorder where the child has difficulty with volitional (voluntary) movement for the production of speech. This can be at the level of sounds, syllables, words, or even phrases (connected speech). The motor struggle is most typically seen with sound sequencing. A speech-language pathologist can offer an in-depth explanation of CAS. (More information is provided in Appendix D.)

CCC—Certificate of Clinical Competence. Being "certified" means holding the Certificate of Clinical Competence (CCC), a nationally recognized professional credential that represents a level of excellence in the field of Audiology (CCC-A) or Speech-Language Pathology (CCC-SLP). Those who have achieved the CCC-ASHA certification have met rigorous academic and professional standards set by the American Speech-Language-Hearing Association. They have the knowledge, skills, and expertise to provide high quality clinical services, and they actively engage in ongoing professional development to keep their certification current.

Cleft Lip and Palate—Cleft lip and cleft palate are openings or splits in the upper lip, the roof of the mouth (palate) or both. Cleft lip and cleft palate result when developing facial structures in an unborn baby don't close completely. In most cases, a series of surgeries can restore normal function and achieve a more normal appearance with minimal scarring. Speech development can be affected by cleft lip and palate. It is important to consult with a speech-language pathologist soon after a cleft lip and/or palate is diagnosed.

Cognition/Cognitive Skills—Cognitive skills may also be referred to as intellectual abilities. When a child has difficulties in cognitive skill development, these limitations will cause a child to learn and develop more slowly than a typical child. Children with cognitive disabilities may take longer to learn to speak, walk, and take care of their personal needs such as dressing or eating.

CP—Cerebral Palsy. CP is a condition caused by injury to parts of the brain that control our ability to use our muscles and bodies. Cerebral means having to do with the brain. Palsy means weakness or problems with using the muscles. Often the injury happens before birth, sometimes during delivery, and sometimes soon after being born. CP can be mild, moderate, or severe. Mild CP may mean a child is clumsy. Moderate CP may mean the child walks with a limp or needs a special leg brace. More severe CP can affect all parts of a child's physical abilities. Sometimes children with CP also have learning problems, problems with hearing or vision, problems with speech or language, or problems with intellectual development. CP does not get worse over time, and most children with CP have a normal life span.

DCD—Developmental Cognitive Disability. DCD is defined as a condition that results in intellectual functioning significantly below average and is associated with concurrent deficits in adaptive behavior that require special education and related services.

DD—Developmental Delay. Via a comprehensive evaluation, this is a label given to children who demonstrate weakness in developing skills in one or more of the following areas: physical development (fine motor skills, gross motor skills), cognitive development (intellectual abilities), communication development (speech and language), social or emotional development (social skills, emotional control), or adaptive development (self-care skills).

DHH—Deaf and Hard of Hearing. Hearing loss is generally described as slight, mild, moderate, severe or profound, depending upon how well a person can hear the intensities (loudness) or frequencies (pitches) most strongly associated with speech. Impairments in hearing can occur in either area and in one or both ears. Hearing loss and deafness can be either acquired (occurring after birth) or congenital (present at birth). Common causes of acquired hearing loss include: exposure to noise; build up of fluid behind the eardrum; ear infections; childhood diseases such as mumps, measles, or chicken pox; and head trauma. Congenital causes include: a family history of loss or deafness; infections during pregnancy; and complications during pregnancy. Hearing loss or deafness may also be a characteristic of another disability such as Down syndrome, Usher syndrome, or Treacher Collins syndrome. In all cases, early detection and treatment are very important to a child's development. DHH teachers specialize in addressing the needs of children with all levels and types of hearing loss.

DS—Down Syndrome. Down syndrome is the most common and readily identifiable chromosomal condition associated with intellectual disabilities. People with Down syndrome are born with 47 chromosomes in some or all of their cells instead of the usual 46 chromosomes. This extra chromosome changes the orderly development of the body and brain. In most cases, the diagnosis of DS is made according to results from a chromosome test administered shortly after birth. There are over fifty clinical signs of Down syndrome, but it is rare to find all or even most of them in one person. Every child with DS is different. Some of the common characteristics include: low muscle tone; slanting eyes with folds of skin at the inner corners; hyper-flexibility; short stature; smaller, lower-set ears; frequent ear infections that can result in conductive hearing loss; smaller, sometimes irregularly shaped teeth that may erupt in an unusual sequence; a mouth that may be small in relationship to the size of the tongue.

DSM—Diagnostic and Statistical Manual of Mental Disorders. The DSM is the standard classification of mental disorders used by mental health professionals in the US. The DSM-V is due for publication in 2013 and will replace the DSM-IV, last revised in 2000.

Due Process—Due process is intended to ensure that children with learning disabilities and other types of disabilities receive a free appropriate public education. These policies and procedures are typically described in a school district's procedural safeguards statement and local policies. Procedural safeguards are sometimes referred to as parent rights statements.

EBD—Emotional-Behavioral Disturbance/Disorder. IDEA defines emotional-behavioral disturbance as follows: "…a condition exhibiting one or more of the following characteristics over a long period of time and to a marked degree that adversely affects a child's educational performance: (a) an inability to learn that cannot be explained by intellectual, sensory, or health factors; (b) an inability to build or maintain satisfactory interpersonal relationships with peers and teachers; (c) inappropriate types of behavior or feelings under normal circumstances; (d) a general pervasive mood of unhappiness or depression; (e) a tendency to develop physical symptoms or fears associated with personal or school problems."

ECFE—Early Childhood Family Education. A program for families with young children who have not yet entered kindergarten, with a focus on strengthening families and enhancing the ability of parents to support their child's learning and development.

Echolalia—Automatic repetition of a word or phrase. Echolalia can be a symptom of a disorder, such as when a person with autism repeats TV commercials, favorite movie scripts, or parental reprimands.

ECSE—Early Childhood Special Education. Early childhood special education addresses the needs of young children with developmental delays. ECSE teachers are specialists who help infants, toddlers, and small children who have learning difficulties or physical disabilities.

Eligibility—Before a child can receive special education and related services for the first time, a full and individual initial evaluation of the child must be conducted to see if the child has a disability and is eligible (according to IDEA) for special education.

ELL/ESL/LEP/ESOL—These acronyms refer to English Language Learners, English as a Second Language, Limited English Proficient, and English for Speakers of Other Languages.

ENT—Ear, Nose, and Throat Specialist. An ENT is a physician trained in the medical and surgical treatment of the ears, nose, throat, and related structures of the head and neck.

Epilepsy—Epilepsy is a seizure disorder. According to the Epilepsy Foundation of America, a seizure happens when a brief, strong surge of electrical activity affects part or all of the brain. Seizures can last from a few seconds to a few minutes. They can have different symptoms, too, from convulsions and loss of consciousness, to signs such as blank staring, lip smacking, or jerking movements of arms and legs.

Some people can have a seizure and yet not have epilepsy. For example, many young children have convulsions from fevers. Other types of seizures not classified as epilepsy include those caused by an imbalance of body fluids or chemicals or by alcohol or drug withdrawal. Thus, a single seizure does not mean that the person has epilepsy. Generally speaking, the diagnosis of epilepsy is made when a person has two or more unprovoked seizures.

ER—Evaluation Report. An evaluation carried out by a child's IEP team along with parent input that uses a variety of assessment tools and strategies to gather relevant functional, developmental, and academic information about the child for the purpose of determining eligibility for special education services. A full and individual evaluation includes evaluating the child's health, vision and hearing, social and emotional status, general intelligence, academic performance, communicative status, and motor abilities.

ESY—Extended School Year. The IEP team considers whether or not a child needs to receive services beyond the typical school year. This is called Extended School Year or ESY services.

FAPE—Free Appropriate Public Education. IDEA defined this term as special education and related services that (a) are provided at public expense, under public supervision and direction, and without charge; (b) meet the standards of the SEA, including the requirements of this part; (c) include an appropriate preschool, elementary school, or secondary school education in the State involved; and (d) are provided in conformity with an individualized education program (IEP) that meets the requirements of §§300.320 through 300.324.

FASD—Fetal Alcohol Spectrum Disorders. This term describes a continuum of permanent birth defects caused by maternal consumption of alcohol during pregnancy.

FERPA—Family Educational Rights and Privacy Act. This is a federal law designed to protect the privacy of a student's education records. These rights transfer from the parents to the student when he or she reaches the age of eighteen or attends a school beyond the high school level.

Fine Motor—Fine motor refers to movements that require a high degree of control and precision. These may include such movements as isolating a finger to point, holding a crayon to color, manipulating puzzle pieces, or using eating utensils.

Gross Motor—Gross motor refers to movements that involve large muscle groups and are generally more broad and energetic than fine motor movements. These may include walking, kicking, jumping, and climbing stairs.

IDEA—Individuals with Disabilities Education Act. Congress originally enacted IDEA in 1975 to ensure that children with disabilities have the opportunity to receive a free appropriate public education, just like other children. The law has been revised many times over the years. Congress passed the most recent amendments in December 2004, August 2006, and September 2011.

IEP—Individualized Education Program. An IEP is a written statement of individualized educational goals and objectives for a child with a disability aged three to twenty-one that is developed, reviewed, and revised in regularly scheduled meetings in keeping with certain requirements of law and regulations.

IFSP—Individualized Family Service Plan. The IFSP is a written document that, among other things, outlines the early intervention services that your child and family will receive. One guiding principal of the IFSP is that the family is a child's greatest resource; that a young child's needs are closely tied to the needs of his or her family. The best way to support children and meet their needs is to support and build upon the individual strengths of their family.

Involvement of other team members will depend on what the child needs. These other team members could come from several agencies and may include medical professionals, therapists, child development specialists, social workers, and so forth. Each state has specific guidelines for the IFSP.

Inclusion—Under the inclusion model, students with special needs spend most or all of their time with non-disabled students. This model ensures that necessary supports and services are provided so children with disabilities can participate with children who are not disabled in school, community, and recreation activities.

LD—Learning Disability. A neurobiological condition that interferes with a person's ability to store, process, or produce information. The skills most often affected are: reading, writing, listening, thinking, speaking, reasoning, and doing math.

LRE—Least Restrictive Environment. In basic terms, LRE refers to the setting where a child with a disability can receive an appropriate education designed to meet his or her educational needs, alongside peers without disabilities to the maximum extent appropriate.

Milestone—A developmental milestone is an ability that is achieved by most children by a certain age. Developmental milestones can involve physical, social, emotional, cognitive, and communication skills such as walking, sharing with others, expressing emotions, recognizing familiar sounds, and talking.

OHI—Other Health Impairment. One of the fourteen categories of disability listed under IDEA that likely qualifies an individual for special services. IDEA states that OHI means having limited strength, vitality, or alertness, including a heightened alertness to environmental stimuli, that results in limited alertness with respect to the educational environment, that - (a) Is due to chronic or acute health problems such as asthma, attention deficit disorder or attention deficit hyperactivity disorder, diabetes, epilepsy, a heart condition, hemophilia, lead poisoning, leukemia, nephritis, rheumatic fever, sickle cell anemia, and Tourette syndrome; and (b) adversely affects a child's educational performance.

Oral Motor—Relating to the muscles of the mouth and/or mouth movements such as sucking, blowing, and chewing.

Orthopedic—The branch of medicine that deals with the prevention or correction of injuries or disorders of the skeletal system and associated muscles, joints, and ligaments. In the school system, an orthopedic impairment means a severe orthopedic impairment that adversely affects a child's educational performance. The term includes impairments caused by a congenital anomaly, impairments caused by disease, and impairments from other causes (e.g., cerebral palsy, fractures).

OT—Occupational Therapy/Therapist. In simple terms, occupational therapists help people participate in the things they want and need to do through the therapeutic use of everyday activities (occupations). Common occupational therapy interventions include helping children with disabilities to participate fully in school and social situations. OTs may work with children who have speech delays if their difficulties include oral motor function. Often, an OT and speech pathologist will work together on a co-treatment plan, each offering their expertise to meet the individual needs of the child.

Paraprofessional (Para)—Someone who works under the supervision of a professional staff member who is responsible for the overall management of a student's program area.

PCA—Personal Care Assistant/Attendant. A PCA is a paid, employed person who helps persons who are disabled or chronically ill with their activities of daily living.

PECS—Picture Exchange Communication System. An augmentative/alternative communication system that teaches individuals with communication deficits to initiate communication using picture symbols. PECS begins by teaching an individual to give a picture of a desired item to a "communicative partner," who immediately honors the exchange as a request. The system goes on to teach discrimination of pictures and how to put them together in sentences. In the more advanced phases, individuals are taught to answer questions and to comment.

PLEP—Present Level of Educational Performance. On an IEP, a statement of the child's present level of functional performance. This includes how the child's disability affects his/her participation in school.

Procedural Safeguards (Parental Rights)—The Notice of Procedural Safeguards is a document that explains the rights of children with IFSPs or IEPs and their parents. It also explains the IFSP and IEP procedure, and how each step plays out.

PT—Physical Therapy/Therapist. Physical therapy is a type of treatment you may need when health problems make it hard to move around and do everyday tasks. Depending on a person's needs, the PT will help with flexibility, strength, endurance, coordination, and/or balance. PTs may work with children who have speech delays if they also have gross motor issues. A child needs to have trunk and neck strength and good head control to coordinate the muscles of the mouth for talking. A PT works with the child to build core strength, which is a foundation for the refined movements needed for talking.

School Psychologist—School psychologists are educated in psychology, child and adolescent development, and family and parenting practices. They are knowledgeable about effective instruction and effective schools. They are trained to carry out psychological assessment, counseling, and consultation.

SI—Sensory Integration. The neurological process that organizes information received through the sensory systems: vision, hearing, smelling, tasting, touch, balance and movement, and position determined by input to the muscles and joints. When a child has a SI difficulty, he does not properly receive sensory input or process the input in a satisfactory way. This causes problems in daily functioning and can often be mistaken for behavioral problems. Children diagnosed with autism often have SI difficulties.

SLP—Speech-Language Pathologist. A specialist who evaluates and treats patients of all ages—from infants to the elderly—with speech, language, cognitive-communication, and swallowing disorders. Speech pathologists have a master's degree or doctorate in their specialty, as well as a Certificate of Clinical Competence (CCC) earned by working under supervision. Some states in the US also require an SLP to earn a state license. SLPs may also be referred to as clinicians or therapists.

Social/Emotional/Behavior Skills—Healthy development of social, emotional, and behavior skills results in a child's ability to express his ideas and feelings, display empathy towards others, manage his feelings of frustration and disappointment more easily, feel self-confident, make friends, and succeed in school.

Spina Bifida—Spina bifida is a birth defect that occurs during the first month or so of pregnancy wherein a portion of the baby's neural tube fails to develop or close properly, causing defects in the spinal cord and in the bones of the backbone. Damage to the nerves and the spinal cord may result. If a child with spina bifida is found eligible for early intervention services (and most are), staff works with the child's family to develop an Individualized Family Services Plan, or IFSP. The IFSP will describe the child's unique needs as well as the services he or she will receive to address those needs.

TBI—Traumatic Brain Injury. TBI is an acquired injury to the brain caused by an external physical force, resulting in a disability that adversely affects a child's educational performance. The term applies to open or closed head injuries resulting in impairments in one or more areas, such as cognition; language; memory; attention; reasoning; abstract thinking; judgment; problem-solving; sensory, perceptual, and motor abilities; psychosocial behavior; physical functions; information processing; and speech. The term does not apply to brain injuries that are congenital or degenerative, or to brain injuries induced by birth trauma.

Appendix B: Delay vs. Disorder

You may hear the terms *delay* and *disorder* and ask, "What's the difference?" A child with a developmental *delay* learns skills at a slower than expected rate but progress occurs in the anticipated sequence (or in an orderly, predictable manner). A child with a developmental *disorder* learns skills out of the typical order. Progress occurs in a disordered pattern. The child has gaps in her achievement of developmental milestones. For instance, a child with a developmental disorder may not attain the milestone of playing pat-a-cake or peek-a-boo but displays the ability to identify letters and numbers before age two.

Developmental disorders can occur across all developmental domains: gross motor, fine motor, cognition (problem-solving), communication, social, and adaptive behavior. It is important to seek professional guidance whenever you are concerned about any aspect of a child's development.

Treatment strategies will differ depending upon the nature of the speech problem. If a child is suspected of having a delay only, intervention will focus on teaching and building upon the next skills expected in typical speech development. If the child is suspected of having a disordered pattern to learning language, intervention will focus on teaching the "missed" skills in order for the child to build a firm foundation for learning new skills. Children with a developmental language disorder require special instruction to address their unique way of learning. This may involve teaching them concrete strategies for interacting socially and utilizing visual supports, for example.

A child with a developmental disorder may also have developmental delays. For children who present with both a speech disorder and delay, intervention will focus on addressing the "missing" skills while ensuring the child is exposed to the typical language sequence of development. Whether a child demonstrates a delay in gaining skills or shows an out-of-order pattern of learning or both, experts recognize the importance of early diagnosis and intervention to improve long-term outcomes.

Early intervention may include the following:
- family training, counseling, and home visits
- speech-language pathology services (sometimes referred to as speech therapy)
- audiology services (hearing impairment services)
- occupational therapy
- physical therapy
- psychological services; medical services (for diagnostic or evaluation purposes)
- health services needed to enable your child to benefit from the other services
- social work services
- assistive technology devices and services
- transportation
- nutrition services
- service coordination services

Appendix C: Speech vs. Language—There Is a Difference

When a child is not talking at the level expected for his age, we say he has a speech-language delay or disorder. What does that really mean? Let's take a closer look.

Expressive Language Delay/Disorder

This term is used to describe the condition of a child who is not *talking* at the level expected for her age. Some signs of a language problem include:

- Not using words to communicate. May use gestures to get needs met, or be very self-reliant or easily frustrated.
- Using some words, but not putting words together to make sentences.
- Not using parts of speech well (i.e., making grammatical errors such as not using plurals, not adding "ing," not using or misusing pronouns or other smaller parts of speech).
- Not having a large vocabulary; i.e., the child does not know the names of many things.
- Knowing the names of things but having trouble "finding" the words—we might say, "It is on the tip of my tongue." This is a word-finding or memory problem.
- Perhaps talking with words and in sentences but not *using* language well to interact with others.

Speech Delay/Disorder

This term refers to the condition wherein a child has difficulty making the *sounds* of speech. He may have difficulty imitating sounds or words or he may have difficulty making specific sounds. Some common reasons for a speech problem include:

- *Hearing loss.* A child may have a permanent hearing loss requiring hearing aids or cochlear implants to assist hearing. A child may have a temporary or fluctuating hearing loss (comes and goes) due to middle ear infection, fluid, excess wax, or structural problem. Children may not hear the sounds clearly or at all, so they do not imitate them correctly. Note: Hearing loss can also cause a language delay.

- *Weak muscles.* Children may not have enough strength or control of the mouth muscles to speak clearly. They may drool and have their mouths open at rest. They may sound like they are mumbling. This is referred to as dysarthria. Note: Drooling can occur due to colds and congestion or teething, and is a normal part of development for babies who explore toys with their mouths.

- *Trouble imitating and sequencing sound patterns.* Sometimes muscles are strong but the problem is that the child cannot easily imitate the motor sequence of sounds to make words. They hear the words just fine, their brains make sense of the information, but there is a breakdown when they try to imitate the words they hear. They have difficulty sequencing the sound patterns to make words. This is referred to as childhood apraxia of speech (CAS). (See Appendix D for more information.)

- *Trouble following the sound rules.* The English language has many "rules" for speech sounds (also known as phonological processes). Children have to learn these rules and all children universally break these rules as they learn to talk. By the age of three, most children are following the sound rules most of the time. When a child fails to gain command over the sound rules on his own, he may need some help to learn the rules. The more sound rules a child breaks, the more difficult his speech is to understand. A child with ongoing concerns in this area is said to have a phonological processing disorder.

The following are examples of sound rules:

- Our words have sounds at the beginning and at the end. Rule breaker: Leave off final or beginning sounds. Children universally simplify words, e.g., *mom* becomes "ma" or *pig* becomes "pi" or *candy* becomes "andy."
- Our words have sound clusters (two or more consonants together, e.g., SN, ST, TR, PL, STR). Rule breaker: Simplify clusters. A young child says "poon" for *spoon* or "pease" for *please* or "tar" for *star*.
- Our words have many syllables. Rule breaker: Simplify syllables. The child calls a *hamburger* a "ham-ger" or a *computer* a "puter" or a *banana* a "nana."

- Our words have airflow sounds (s, sh, f, th). Rule breaker: Stopping the airflow. Children often stop the airflow sounds in words that require them, saying, for example, "knipe" for *knife*, "toup" for *soup*, "du" for *shoe*, and "dis" for *this*.
- Our words have "places," e.g., we make K, G, and NG sounds in the back of the throat. Rule breaker: Fronting. This is substituting sounds in words that are made in the back of the throat with easier sounds that are made at the front of the mouth. A child will say "tup" for *cup*, or "doe" for *go*, or "win" for *wing*.

Treatment depends upon the identified problem. A child may have an expressive language problem and a speech problem at the same time. The speech-language pathologist can help determine the area(s) of most concern. The speech-language pathologist (also called speech therapist, speech clinician) can help families help their children learn to communicate to their fullest potential.

Appendix D: Childhood Apraxia of Speech

Why can't my child imitate what I ask him to say?

Early on, children learn to put meaning to the sounds they make. They coo and babble and inadvertently say things like "ma-mama" or "bah boh" or "adadada." When we hear infants and toddlers making these sounds we impose meaning and say, "Oh, listen! He just said *mama*!" or "I think she just said *bubble*!"

Over time, children will associate sound combinations with words and will gain the ability to imitate speech. When they are able to maturely imitate speech, they say their first words. This happens for most children around their first birthday.

When children have difficulty imitating speech sounds, they may not babble as much. They may not get as much practice with speech sounds. And they may not get as much reinforcement from caregivers. This can lead to a delay in talking.

When a child has significant difficulty forming, sequencing, and imitating speech-motor patterns it may be categorized as childhood apraxia of speech, or CAS. Children with CAS have difficulty imitating speech sound patterns. It is especially hard for them to imitate on command. They may be able to say "mama" when they are playing on their own, but when asked to repeat it, they cannot. This becomes frustrating for everyone—especially the child!

To help a child improve his ability to imitate sounds and words, we often need to step back and return to the earlier levels of pre-speech development where caregivers and children simply play with sounds and where the caregiver takes the child's lead and diminishes the pressure on the child to talk. When the difficulty is severe, a speech pathologist can provide more specific intervention ideas. (See Tips and Techniques: No Pressure Practice on page 30.)

Appendix E: Functional Communication

When selecting words and signs to teach a young child, think function. There are four main reasons for communication: to express wants and needs; to build social closeness (build relationships); to exchange information (ask and answer questions); and to fulfill social rules for etiquette. Ask yourself what words will provide the child ways to meet those four functions. Avoid spending a lot of time teaching colors, shapes, numbers, and letters until the child has a solid core vocabulary to meet her needs.

Considering the four areas of communicative function, what does a young child need to tell us?

- Pay attention to me (Mommy, Daddy, Grandma, etc.)!
- I am hungry.
- I am thirsty.
- I need help.
- I want more.
- Do that again!
- I am all done.
- I want to go in/out/up/down/bye-bye/store/ school/home, etc.
- I love you.
- Let's play!
- Me, too!
- I need you (Mommy, Daddy, etc.).
- I have a poopy/messy diaper.

- I have an "owie" (and where, such as tummy, ear).
- I want some food/toy/other item.
- I want you to come/go/read/sit/hug/etc.
- No!
- Yes!
- I am sticky/dirty (wash me).
- It is broken (help fix).
- Turn light on/off (or let me do it).
- Look at what I am interested in (bus, snow, animal in the book, etc.).
- What's that? (I want to know what that is called).
- Where is Daddy/Mommy/Grandpa/Grandma/etc.?
- This is mine!
- Stop doing that!
- I need my hat/coat/shoes/boots/blanket/etc.
- Sorry.
- Please.
- Thank you.
- Hi!
- Bye-bye!

Select signs and words that hold the power to communicate important wants and needs. Add in words for colors, numbers, shapes, letters, zoo animals, and vehicle names, as well. Just be sure to focus first on function!

Appendix F: List of Words Used Frequently by Toddlers

One of the first questions a doctor or speech therapist may ask a parent who has concerns about her child's talking/speech is, "How many words does he say?" Parents are often at a loss to come up with a number, and often underestimate their child's working vocabulary.

The following list of words commonly used by toddlers (in no particular order) is a good place to start to accurately tally up your child's words. Some of the words are simplified to assist you in crediting your youngster with his version of a word. Children often simplify their words ("blanket" becomes *banky*, for example) and parents are sometimes reluctant to count these simple utterances as "words." It is extremely helpful for speech therapists to know everything the child says, even if it is "sh" for *quiet* or "heh heh" for a panting dog.

- More
- Again or "Gen"
- Help
- Please
- Thank you
- Hi
- Goodbye or "Bye-bye"
- Uh-oh
- Yes or "Uh-huh"
- No or "Uh-uh"
- Eat
- Drink
- Milk
- Juice
- Water or "Wah-wah"
- Bottle or "Bah-bah"
- Go
- Horse or "Horsey"
- Mama
- Dada
- Baby
- Papa (Grandpa)
- Dig
- Car
- Names of siblings, friends, pets
- Nice
- Owie
- Yeah
- Kiss
- Hug
- Tickle
- Give me or "Gimme"
- Oops
- Sorry
- Stop
- All done
- Up (Lift me)
- Goodnight or "Nigh-nigh"
- Open
- Want
- Down (Get down)
- Icky or "Ishy"
- Hot
- Cold
- Me
- Mine
- You
- I
- Ball
- Book
- Diaper
- Sock
- C'mon (Come)
- Do
- Bus
- Movie/Show (or name of show)
- Mama (Grandma)
- Out
- Toes
- Eyes
- Mouth
- Nose
- Tummy/Belly
- Bubble
- Pop-pop
- Poopy
- Pee pee
- Wash

- Love you
- Shoe
- Coat
- Hat
- Chair
- Table
- Bed
- Blanket or "Banky"
- Light
- Cookie
- Cracker
- Cheese
- Apple
- Banana
- Nuk®
- Dog/Puppy
- Cat/Kitty
- Cow
- What's that? or "Whassat?"
- Peek/Boo
- Sit
- Hide
- Music (or name of song)
- Boom
- Spoon
- Cup

- Cut
- Look
- Store
- School
- Want
- Off
- On
- Broken
- (Animal sounds)

Appendix G: Developmental Milestones of Typically Developing Children—First 12 Months

The following list of milestones is a means to track the progress of a child's growth and development. It can help you determine if and when to consult your child's pediatrician or a specialist, such as a speech therapist or an early childhood special education teacher.

Not all children will meet the milestones on a typical timeline. Children with Down syndrome, for example, may need more time and specialized instruction to reach certain milestones. Some children with significant motor impairment may not master certain motor skills without assistance.

This list is meant as a guide only. It is a way to track development, monitor progress, and alert you to potential issues. It is not intended to diagnose a problem or replace a developmental screening or evaluation by a qualified professional. But if your child is not meeting the milestones for his age, or if you have any concerns about the way the child plays, learns, talks, or behaves, don't hesitate to speak with a professional. That's what they're there for.

By 3 months of age

Motor Skills
- Lift head when held at your shoulder
- Lift head and chest when lying on his stomach
- Turn head from side to side when lying on his stomach
- Follow a moving object or person with his eyes
- Grasp rattle when given to her
- Wiggle and kick with arms and legs

Sensory and Thinking Skills
- Turn head toward bright colors and lights
- Turn toward the sound of a human voice
- Recognize bottle or breast
- Respond to your shaking a rattle or bell

Language and Social Skills
- Make cooing, gurgling sounds
- Smile when smiled at
- Communicate hunger, fear, discomfort (through crying or facial expression)
- Usually quiets down at the sound of a soothing voice or when held

By 6 months of age

Motor Skills
- Hold head steady when sitting with your help
- Reach for and grasp objects
- Play with his toes
- Help hold the bottle during feeding
- Explore by mouthing and banging objects
- Move toys from one hand to another
- Pull up to a sitting position on her own if you grasp her hands
- Sit with only a little support
- Roll over
- Bounce when held in a standing position

Sensory and Thinking Skills

- Open his mouth for the spoon
- Imitate familiar actions you perform

Language and Social Skills

- Babble, making almost sing-song sounds
- Know familiar faces
- Laugh and squeal with delight
- Scream if annoyed
- Smile at herself in a mirror

By 12 months of age

Motor Skills

- Drink from a cup with help
- Feed herself finger food, like raisins
- Grasp small objects by using her thumb and index or forefinger
- Use his first finger to poke or point
- Put small blocks in and take them out of a container
- Knock two blocks together
- Sit well without support
- Crawl on hands and knees
- Pull himself to stand or take steps holding onto furniture
- Stand alone momentarily
- Walk with one hand held

Sensory and Thinking Skills

- Copy sounds and actions you make
- Respond to music with body motion
- Try to accomplish simple goals (seeing and then crawling to a toy)
- Look for an object she watched fall out of sight (such as a spoon that falls under the table)

Language and Social Skills

- Babble, but it sometimes "sounds like" talking
- Say his first word
- Recognize family members' names
- Try to "talk" with you
- Respond to another's distress by showing distress or crying
- Show affection to familiar adults
- Show apprehension about strangers
- Raise her arms when she wants to be picked up
- Understand simple commands

Note: If you'd like to know more about what experts consider the developmental milestones for children older than one year, resource links are provided at the National Dissemination Center for Children with Disabilities website: http://nichcy.org.

Source: *National Dissemination Center for Children with Disabilities, 1825 Connecticut Ave. NW, Washington, DC 20009*

Appendix H: Recommended Resources

The American Speech-Language-Hearing Association—www.Asha.org

This group is committed to ensuring that all people with speech, language, and hearing disorders receive services to help them communicate effectively. Its mission is to empower and support speech-language pathologists, audiologists, and speech, language, and hearing scientists.

ASHAsphere—www.Blog.Asha.org

The official blog of the American Speech-Language-Hearing Association, this blog is intended to inspire discussion about issues related to the fields of audiology and speech pathology, and features posts from a variety of authors.

Autism Speaks—www.Autismspeaks.org

A leading autism science and advocacy organization, dedicated to funding research into the causes, prevention, treatments, and a cure for autism, increasing awareness of autism spectrum disorders, and advocating for the needs of individuals with autism and their families.

Baby Talk

Baby Talk is a free, one-way listserv that is distributed every other week. Each issue features one or more resources, the majority of which are available to download at no cost. To join the listserv, send an email with no message to subscribe-babytalk@listserv.unc.edu.

The Big Book of Exclamations by Teri Kaminski-Peterson M.S. CCC/SLP—www.Thebigbookofexclamations.com

A fun, educational book designed to promote speech sound development, and imitation of gestures, sounds, and words.

The Childhood Apraxia of Speech Association of North America (CASANA) and **Apraxia-KIDS**—www.Apraxia-Kids.org

This group's mission is to strengthen the support systems in the lives of children with apraxia, so that each child has his best opportunity to develop speech.

First Signs—www.Firstsigns.org

This nonprofit national organization is dedicated to educating parents and professionals about the early warning signs of autism and related disorders. Their mission is to ensure the best developmental outcome for every child by promoting awareness regarding the most important and often overlooked aspects of development: social, emotional, and communication.

HOPE—http://hope.cochlearamericas.com

A website established to assist children with cochlear implants, it also contains a wealth of information for the speech-language pathologist working with young children with or without a hearing loss. Free documents include interactive tools, games, and printable PDF exercises. They also have an app called HOPEWords designed to improve the listening and spoken language skills of children with hearing loss.

KIZCLUB—www.Kizclub.com

This site provides lots of educational activities in language arts for preschool and elementary age children.

Marshalla Speech & Language—www.Pammarshalla.com

This site is devoted to providing practical, high-quality, and common-sense resources for speech-language pathologists and parents.

National Dissemination Center for Children with Disabilities—www.Nichcy.org

Serving the nation as a central source of information on disabilities in infants, toddlers, children, and youth. They provide numerous links to medical and educational research and news.

Noisy Stories: Language Activities for Children of All Communicative Abilities by Joan Rivard, M.A./CCC-SLP and Jessica Rivard—www.Mayer-johnson.com/noisy-stories

Noisy Stories presents sounds in isolation and in combination in a developmentally appropriate format. It encourages children to respond verbally, with a sign, or with an AAC device.

Pinterest—www.Pinterest.com

This site lets you organize and share all the wonderful things you find on the web. Search "speech-language" for lots of resources and ideas for helping your child communicate.

Signing Savvy—www.Signingsavvy.com

Signing Savvy is a sign language dictionary containing several thousand high resolution videos of American Sign Language (ASL) signs, fingerspelled words, and other common signs used within the United States and Canada.

Signing Time—www.Signingtime.com

Signing Time is a labor of love, born out of the desire for one mother to create a community that could communicate with her deaf daughter. Offers a wide range of DVDs to effectively teach sign language to young children and adults.

Speakingofspeech.com—www.Speakingofspeech.com

The first and largest interactive forum for speech-language pathologists and teachers to improve communication skills in our schools by exchanging ideas, techniques, materials, and lessons that work; finding out about materials before you buy; seeking and giving advice on therapy and caseload management issues; and exploring a myriad of helpful resource links.

Speech-language-therapy.com—www.Speech-language-therapy.com

This site's mission is to provide useful, theoretically sound, and, where possible, evidence-based information about human communication disorders.

Starfall.com—www.Starfall.com

A free, public, online service to teach children about sound awareness and early reading.

Talk It Rock It—www.Talkitrockit.com

The home for songs, audio-visual shows, the Push-Pull Puzzle, and many other speech and language enrichment products created by Rachel Arntson, M.S., CCC-SLP.

Talking is Hard for Me—www.Talkingishardforme.com

Resources for parents, caregivers, and professionals on ways to help the child who finds talking difficult. Maintained by speech-language pathologist and author, Linda Reinert, MS., CCC-SLP.

Teach Me to Talk!—www.Teachmetotalk.com

This group is committed to providing quality clinical services for children ages birth to four with communication delays and disorders, developing outstanding "real life" resources to help professionals and parents teach toddlers to understand and use language, and providing a variety of professional development opportunities for speech-language pathologists and other early intervention professionals who assess and provide treatment for young children with developmental delays and disorders.

About the Author

Linda M. Reinert has over twenty-five years experience as a speech-language pathologist working with children ages birth to five. She has worked in a variety of settings including homes, schools, and medical clinics. Reinert gathered the material for this book while working directly with young children and their families. It was the children themselves who inspired her to give them a voice; to allow them to tell you what they want you to know—that you CAN help them communicate! She resides in rural Minnesota.

About the Illustrator

Emily S. Lynch is a painter whose work is rooted in pattern. She received a B.A. in Mathematics from Luther College in 2006, before completing her BFA from the University of Minnesota in 2012. Lynch is a Minnesota State Arts Board Mentorship Grant recipient, and represented the University of Minnesota in the 2011 Undergraduate Student Showcase Show. She currently lives in and works from her studio in Delano, Minnesota.